Hummingbirds

by Megan Borgert-Spaniol

BELLWETHER MEDIA · MINNEAPOLIS, MN

Note to Librarians, Teachers, and Parents:

Blastoff! Readers are carefully developed by literacy experts and combine standards-based content with developmentally appropriate text.

Level 1 provides the most support through repetition of high-frequency words, light text, predictable sentence patterns, and strong visual support.

Level 2 offers early readers a bit more challenge through varied simple sentences, increased text load, and less repetition of high-frequency words.

Level 3 advances early-fluent readers toward fluency through increased text and concept load, less reliance on visuals, longer sentences, and more literary language.

Level 4 builds reading stamina by providing more text per page, increased use of punctuation, greater variation in sentence patterns, and increasingly challenging vocabulary.

Level 5 encourages children to move from "learning to read" to "reading to learn" by providing even more text, varied writing styles, and less familiar topics.

Whichever book is right for your reader, Blastoff! Readers are the perfect books to build confidence and encourage a love of reading that will last a lifetime!

This edition first published in 2014 by Bellwether Media, Inc.

No part of this publication may be reproduced in whole or in part without written permission of the publisher. For information regarding permission, write to Bellwether Media, Inc., Attention: Permissions Department, 5357 Penn Avenue South, Minneapolis, MN 55419.

Library of Congress Cataloging-in-Publication Data

Borgert-Spaniol, Megan, 1989- author.
  Hummingbirds / by Megan Borgert-Spaniol.
    pages cm. – (Blastoff! Readers. Backyard Wildlife)
  Summary: "Developed by literacy experts for students in kindergarten through grade three, this book introduces hummingbirds to young readers through leveled text and related photos"– Provided by publisher.
  Audience: 5-8.
  Audience: Grade K to 3.
  Includes bibliographical references and index.
  ISBN 978-1-62617-059-9 (hardcover : alk. paper)
  1. Hummingbirds–Juvenile literature. I. Title. II. Series: Blastoff! readers. 1, Backyard wildlife.
  QL696.A558B67 2014
  598.7'64–dc23
                              2013032721

Printed in the United States of America, North Mankato, MN.

Contents

What Are Hummingbirds?   4

Flying   10

Finding Food   14

Glossary   22

To Learn More   23

Index   24

Hummingbirds are small, colorful birds. They have long wings and short legs.

Male hummingbirds have colorful **gorgets**. These feathers shine in the light.

gorget

Most hummingbirds live in warm areas. They make their homes in forests, grasslands, and **deserts**.

Hummingbirds can fly forward, backward, and sideways. They also fly upside down.

Hummingbirds also **hover**. They can flap their wings more than 80 times each second.

Hummingbirds stick their long **bills** into flowers. They **lap** up the **nectar** inside.

bill

They also catch
insects in the air.
Sometimes they
eat spiders.

Female hummingbirds bring food to their **nestlings**. They feed the babies from their bills.

Hummingbirds do not like to share. They often fight over flowers. Back off!

Glossary

bills—the hard outer parts of the mouths of birds

deserts—dry lands with little rain

gorgets—patches of feathers on the throats of some birds

hover—to stay in one place in the air

insects—small animals with six legs and hard outer bodies; insect bodies are divided into three parts.

lap—to take in liquid with the tongue

nectar—a sweet liquid that comes from plants

nestlings—baby birds that are too young to leave the nest

To Learn More

AT THE LIBRARY

Collins, Dennis. *Happy Hummingbirds.*
Mustang, Okla.: Tate Publishing, 2008.

Schuetz, Kari. *Birds*. Minneapolis, Minn.:
Bellwether Media, 2013.

Sill, Cathryn P. *About Hummingbirds: A Guide
For Children*. Atlanta, Ga.: Peachtree, 2011.

ON THE WEB

Learning more about
hummingbirds is as easy as 1, 2, 3.

1. Go to www.factsurfer.com.

2. Enter "hummingbirds" into the search box.

3. Click the "Surf" button and you will see a
   list of related Web sites.

With factsurfer.com, finding more information
is just a click away.

Index

bills, 14, 15, 18

birds, 4

colorful, 4, 6

deserts, 8

eat, 16

feathers, 6

feed, 18

female, 18

fight, 20

flowers, 14, 20

fly, 10

forests, 8

gorgets, 6, 7

grasslands, 8

hover, 12

insects, 16

lap, 14

legs, 4

male, 6

nectar, 14

nestlings, 18

spiders, 16

wings, 4, 12

The images in this book are reproduced through the courtesy of: David G. Hemmings/ Getty Images, front cover; Glenn Bartley/ All Canada Photos/ Superstock, p. 5; Tim Zurowksi/ All Canada Photos/ Superstock, pp. 7, 17; Jim Crosswell/ All Canada Photos/ Superstock, p. 9; Juan Martinez, p. 9 (bottom left); Elenamiv, p. 9 (bottom middle); Katrina Leigh, p. 9 (bottom right); William Leaman/ Alamy, p. 11; Mesquite53, p. 13; Pimmimemom, p. 15; noolwlee, p. 17 (bottom left); skynetphoto, p. 17 (bottom right); Frank Pali/ age fotostock/ Superstock, p. 19; Biosphoto/ SuperStock, p. 21.